STATES OF MIND

I FEEL CONFIDENT

BY STEPHANIE FINNE

BLUE OWL BOOKS

TIPS FOR CAREGIVERS

Social and emotional learning (SEL) helps children manage emotions, create and achieve goals, maintain relationships, learn how to feel empathy, and make good decisions. The SEL approach will help children establish positive habits in communication, cooperation, and decision-making. By incorporating SEL in early reading, children will be better equipped to build confidence and foster positive peer networks.

BEFORE READING

Talk to the reader about confidence. Explain that confidence comes from within.

Discuss: What does it feel like when you are confident? What helps you feel confident?

AFTER READING

Talk to the reader about confidence and self-awareness.

Discuss: What are some things you are good at? How does doing those things make you feel? What small goals can you set and achieve to build confidence?

SEL GOAL

Some students may struggle with confidence. They may not be able to see their own strengths. Help readers develop a vocabulary to voice their feelings. Help them learn to stop and think about what they are good at and how that makes them feel. Help build confidence by acknowledging achievements and hard work.

TABLE OF CONTENTS

CHAPTER 1
Confidence Is Key 4

CHAPTER 2
Growing Confidence 10

CHAPTER 3
Spreading Confidence 16

GOALS AND TOOLS
Grow with Goals 22
Try This! 22
Glossary 23
To Learn More 23
Index 24

CHAPTER 1

CONFIDENCE IS KEY

Can you think of a time you felt proud? Maybe it was the time you hit the winning run. Or it could be when you got a perfect score on a quiz. You felt good about yourself. You knew you could do anything if you tried!

Feeling **confident** is believing in your own abilities. When you are confident, you see the good things you can do. You trust in your own skills.

When we are confident, we are comfortable talking to others. We are comfortable feeling heard. Have you seen friends or classmates who are confident? How do they speak and act?

Meg is comfortable speaking in front of the class. How can we tell? She makes eye contact. She smiles. She uses **gestures**.

Confidence shows in our **body language**. It helps some of us walk tall and proud. It helps some of us speak up and look at others when we do.

TRY IT!

Test out your confident body language. Stand up straight with your shoulders back. Keep your chin up. You could even try standing like a superhero! Stand with your feet apart and your hands on your hips. How do you feel?

CHAPTER 2

GROWING CONFIDENCE

Confidence helps build **courage** to try new things. It also helps you **accept** mistakes. When you are confident, you know you can do anything if you try hard. It took Mark all season to learn how to dive. Now he does it all the time!

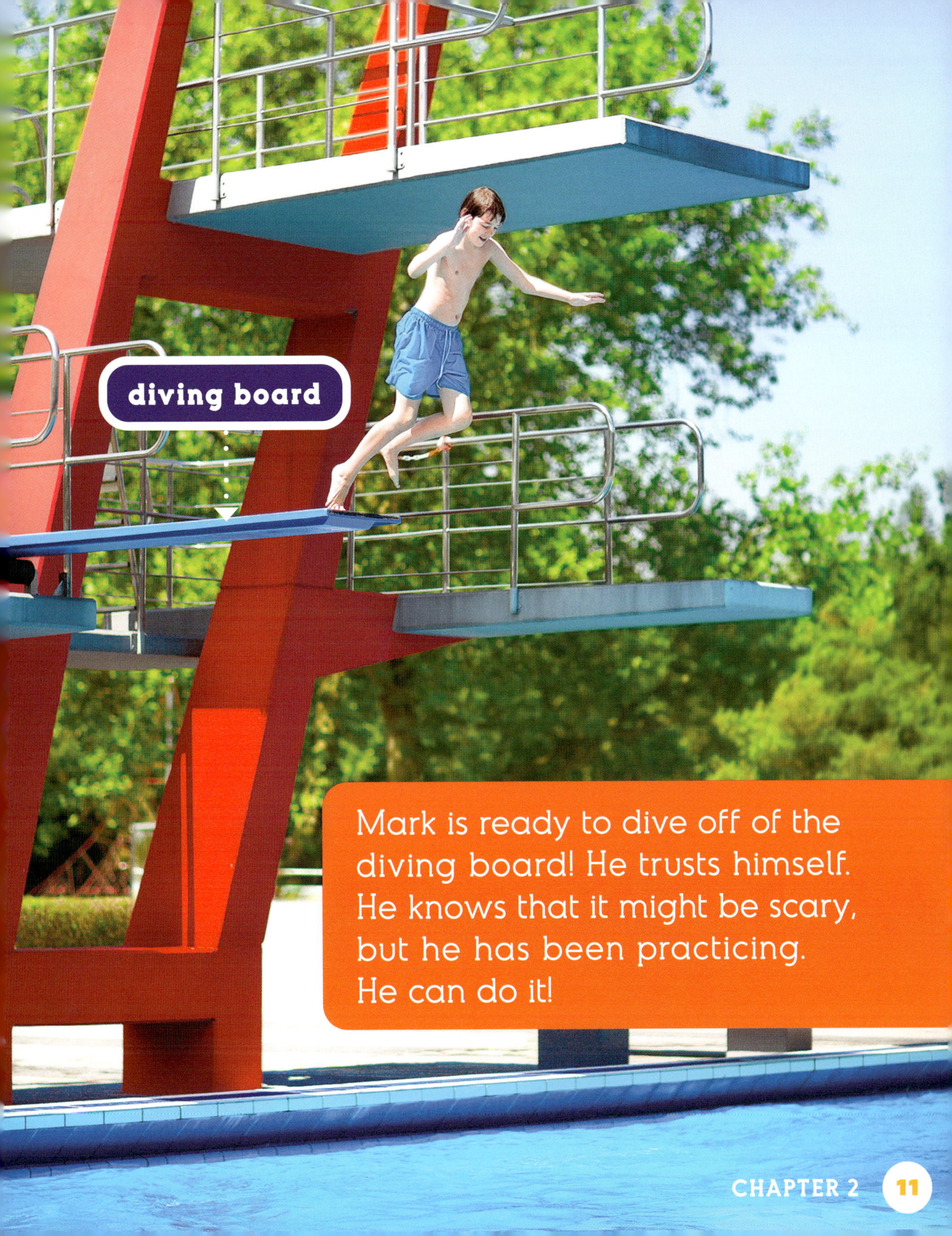

Mark is ready to dive off of the diving board! He trusts himself. He knows that it might be scary, but he has been practicing. He can do it!

One way to build confidence is through meeting **goals**. Steph wants to learn to build a robot on her own. She writes down her goal. She makes a list of steps she has to take to reach it. Then she starts working on them one at a time.

What is a goal you want to reach? Start working on your steps. There will likely be **setbacks**. This is OK! It takes effort to accomplish a goal. Work hard for it! Do not give up when things are difficult. This is called **perseverance**.

TALK WITH CONFIDENCE

You may doubt your abilities, especially if you believe **negative self-talk**. This can sound like, "This is too hard." You may tell yourself you can't do it. If that happens, think positive! Tell yourself, "This is hard, but I can do it!"

CHAPTER 3

SPREADING CONFIDENCE

Sometimes it helps to share your goals. Talk to your friends about what you want to do. Ask them what their goals are. Celebrate when you reach your goals. This will help you all gain confidence.

Think of ways you can do what you are good at every day. Help friends or classmates find what they are good at. You can always work on growing your confidence.

Maya and Tammy want to grow confidence in their **community**. They help clean up the beach. Doing kind things feels good. They see how their work helps. It is another way to spread confidence to the world.

When you are confident, you feel good about yourself. You want to help others feel the same way. You can spread confidence! How will you do it?

BELIEVE IN YOURSELF

Close your eyes. Take a deep breath. Imagine yourself doing something you are nervous to do. Feel how proud you are when it's done. This helps you build confidence in yourself. You can do it!

GOALS AND TOOLS

GROW WITH GOALS

Confidence is something that grows. Try these goals to help build your confidence!

Goal: Make a list of things you are good at! These are your strengths. Realizing your strengths can help you feel confident.

Goal: Dream big! Make a list of goals you want to achieve. Write them down, along with the steps you need to take to achieve those goals.

Goal: Try making a goal ladder! Draw a picture of a ladder with rungs. Write your goal on the top rung. Start at the bottom and work your way up, writing down the steps you will take to reach your goal.

TRY THIS!

Part of feeling confident comes from identifying our emotions. Try using stories to identify your feelings.

1. Think of a character in a book who was afraid to try something but was brave and confident enough to face the challenge.
2. Have you ever had the same feelings as the character?
3. Write down or draw how you handled the same feelings.
4. Discuss your drawing with a parent or teacher. Show and tell them how you felt.

GLOSSARY

accept
To agree that something is correct, satisfactory, or enough.

body language
The gestures, movements, and mannerisms by which people communicate with others.

community
A group of people who all have something in common.

confident
Self-assured and having a strong belief in your own abilities.

courage
Bravery, or the ability to do something that scares you.

gestures
Actions that show feelings.

goals
Things you aim to do.

negative self-talk
Words or thoughts to yourself that cause you to doubt yourself or your abilities and that limit your ability to believe in yourself.

perseverance
Persistence in doing or trying something, even if you have difficulties.

setbacks
Problems that delay you or keep you from making progress.

TO LEARN MORE

FACT SURFER

Finding more information is as easy as 1, 2, 3.

1. Go to www.factsurfer.com
2. Enter "**Ifeelconfident**" into the search box.
3. Choose your cover to see a list of websites.

INDEX

abilities 5, 15
body language 8
celebrate 16
classmates 7, 17
comfortable 7
community 19
courage 10
doubt 15
effort 15
eye contact 7
friends 7, 16, 17
gestures 7
goals 12, 15, 16
mistakes 10
negative self-talk 15
perseverance 15
practicing 11
proud 4, 8, 20
scary 11
setbacks 15
skills 5
smiles 7
speak 7, 8
steps 12, 15
trust 5, 11
try 8, 10

Blue Owl Books are published by Jump!, 5357 Penn Avenue South, Minneapolis, MN 55419, www.jumplibrary.com

Library of Congress Cataloging-in-Publication Data

Names: Finne, Stephanie, author.
Title: I feel confident / by Stephanie Finne.
Description: Minneapolis: Jump!, Inc., 2021. | Series: States of mind
Includes index. | Audience: Ages 7–10 | Audience: Grades 2–3
Identifiers: LCCN 2019048193 (print)
LCCN 2019048194 (ebook)
ISBN 9781645274018 (hardcover)
ISBN 9781645274025 (paperback)
ISBN 9781645274032 (ebook)
Subjects: LCSH: Emotions in children—Juvenile literature. | Confidence in children—Juvenile literature.
Affective education—Juvenile literature.
Classification: LCC BF723.E6 F56 2021 (print)
LCC BF723.E6 (ebook) | DDC 155.4/124–dc23
LC record available at https://lccn.loc.gov/2019048193
LC ebook record available at https://lccn.loc.gov/2019048194

Editor: Jenna Gleisner
Designer: Molly Ballanger

Photo Credits: Luis Molinero/Shutterstock, cover; JBryson/iStock, 1; Donna Ellen Coleman/Shutterstock, 3; Jupiterimages/Getty, 4; ziggy_mars/Shutterstock, 5; Ariel Skelley/Getty, 6–7; JGI/Jamie Grill/Getty, 8–9; FamVeld/Shutterstock, 10, 11; Georgijevic/iStock, 12–13; p_ponomareva/Shutterstock, 14–15; loco75/iStock, 16; fstop123/iStock, 17; SolStock/iStock, 18–19; praetorianphoto/iStock, 20–21.

Printed in the United States of America at Corporate Graphics in North Mankato, Minnesota.